Whitman/Vitman

poems by

Richard J. Fein

Finishing Line Press
Georgetown, Kentucky

Whitman/Vitman

Copyright © 2019 by Richard J. Fein
ISBN 978-1-64662-102-6 First Edition
All rights reserved under International and Pan-American Copyright Conventions. No part of this book may be reproduced in any manner whatsoever without written permission from the publisher, except in the case of brief quotations embodied in critical articles and reviews.

ACKNOWLEDGMENTS

"A Professor Re-reading Calamus (1967)" appeared in *The Poetry Porch*.
"To Walt Whitman" appeared in the anthology *Visiting Walt* (University of Iowa Press), edited by Sheila Coghill and Thom Tammaro.

The last four poems are new poems, and the rest of the poems appeared in my books over the years.

The bi-centennial of Whitman's birth (2019) prompts me to make a gathering of these poems of mine.

Once again I must thank George Kalogeris, who helped me mold this book and whose presence in my life and work has been vital to me.

Publisher: Leah Maines
Editor: Christen Kincaid
Cover Art: The reproduction of Thomas Eakins's portrait of Walt Whitman on the front cover is used with the permission of the Museum of Fine Arts, Boston.
Author Photo: Stanley Sagov
Cover Design: Elizabeth Maines McCleavy

Printed in the USA on acid-free paper.
Order online: www.finishinglinepress.com
also available on amazon.com

Author inquiries and mail orders:
Finishing Line Press
P. O. Box 1626
Georgetown, Kentucky 40324
U. S. A.

Table of Contents

To Walt Whitman 1

Your Grass 5

If only my mother had eaten Leaves of Grass... 6

Visiting My Father's Grave 9

Streets 10

To America 12

A Born-Again Song of Myself 16

from "Sleep-Chasings" 18

from "The Last Poems of Yankev Rivlin" 19

Whitman at Timber Creek 22

Richard III at the Bowery Theater 23

A Professor Re-reading *Calamus* (1967) 24

Here's Looking at You, Whitman 26

Whitman/Vitman 27

Note 28

For Bert Stern

To Walt Whitman

That old man—tramping down Flatbush Avenue—
with a cane, white beard, light brown tunic
and gray felt trooper hat—that was you—
Walt—just like your picture—when you held court
in Camden—avuncular, garrulous and ruddy—
I was climbing up the avenue—where it runs
between the zoo and the botanical gardens—
one of those "ample hills of Brooklyn"—
Why didn't I follow you? Why didn't I stop
and go back down with you? Something kept me in check
as I hiked toward the library—to finish my thesis
on you—You came to turn me around—there
you were—within a foot of me—here on the streets
we shared—and I missed what you showed me—You knew
that would happen—and encouraged me to look
for you again—that's what your beard proposed—I resisted
your very words I memorized—But missing you there—
I took the long way around to find you again—
In '91—when I quit teaching—never to do a seminar
on you again—I ran to the barber shop to get rid
of my beard—which I hid behind since '67—
Sitting on the big chair before the long mirror—
I saw my father's face—I came out from under my beard—

How do we change—Walt? Do you think poetry
has anything to do with it? Do you think we miss
our chance—the way I walked past you—until we
just get tired of the way we are—slowly ready
ourselves—and when that old man—I mean you—
comes back—find that we follow him? Say, the way you
went south—stopped writing editorials—visited the sick
in the city hospitals—owned up to those affections
churning in you—let out your fears of flesh-betrayals—
found your parallelisms and your lists and possessed your world—

I think of our lives—Walt—and they work something like this—
At Castle Garden—where you heard Jenny Lind sing—
and where my grandparents came through as immigrants—
I saw fishes in the tanks—sea horses with their plated
bodies—their beady eyes and crocodile snouts—standing
up in the sand—like curved musical notes—Tentacles
swayed around the mouths of anemones—and the tails
of fishes flicked as they disappeared in the caves—
I saw all this as a child—holding my father's hand—
We are connected—Walt—through that renovated round
building at the Battery—where I feared the glass
would break and all that sea life—and all that water—
come pouring out—drowning me—the fishes swimming
over me—out into the Upper Bay—through the Narrows—
beyond the mouth of the Hudson—deep into the Atlantic—

I think of our lives—Walt—and they work something like this—
I carried you around in my hip pocket—that old
Boni edition—the forest green cover—leathery—
fitting snugly against my ass—I opened you up
on trolley cars buses ferries the el the subway—
Going to work—traveling to relatives—riding around
to escape my bedroom—I read about naked swimmers—
ants on stalks—splotches of moss and lichen—corpses
in the grass—oceans and pavements that spoke to you—
and that spoke to me the same—as if we were one ear—
I read you in my throat as the train made contact
with the third rail—the trolley with the overhead wire—
as the ferry with the accordion gate steamed to Weehawken—
O Walt—I convinced myself I absorbed you—that motion—
that parturient waiting—that sympathy—that listening
to bird, wave, and the grinder sharpening the knife—
But it took me years and years to get to my poem—
borrowing from you—where I recall I never kissed
my father—Even today when I walk the esplanade

at Brooklyn Heights I think of you and Hart Crane
and Melville—making up a past New York
that dwells in me—Once in '55—during my lunch hour—
not far from the place where Lafayette kissed you
when you were a child—I searched out the corner on Fulton
and Cranberry—and there I saw the plaque on the wall—
above two garbage cans—marking the place—so it's said—
where you and the journeyman set print for the poem you finally
called "Song of Myself"—in your book of voyages and retreats—
Back then I did not know that you could teach me
how to write out of my cave of despair—I couldn't see
how you had emerged—from the dark vaults of yourself—
Many times I missed you—though you were inches away—

I think of our lives—Walt—and they work something like this—
One high school summer I cut and stacked steel piping—
and kept the green bins filled with screws—at Manny's
Hardware off the Bowery—where you went to the theater—
I walked under the el during my lunch hour and saw
how the fractured light linked with its own shadows—
how rails and ties and girders transformed the streets
to a chiaroscuro that spread to hoods and roofs of cars—
to the drunks wavering on the curbs—to the signs and pillars
of lights—to the green roofs over the subway steps—
Squares of pavements oddly glared in front of the dark
vestibule of a store—or where old-timers huddled at an entrance—
You—Walt—and Reginald Marsh and Berenice Abbott and Hopper
encouraged me to trust my hunch—that what I saw
in the colors and lines and angles of the streets—
in the arms of taxi meters—in the valleys of fedoras—
in the toe cleavages peeping from black pumps—in the lead
clamps that secured plates of glass where they meet
at the edges—were recesses of myself—alphabets
to read—fractions of the streets and the shops
lodged in me—Mannahatta-tokens of myself—
Walt—it never dawned on me to walk east

and visit what was left of that Jewish world—
for it took me three decades more to walk *those* streets—
looking for the ghosts of Yiddish writers—entering
the remnants and renovations of their old haunts—
trying to imagine them there—Yet back in '47—
when they were still in the flesh—I walked the other way—
So much so near—I never knew how to grasp—Your book—
Walt—I held it too close to me—and didn't even see
you warned against that—how that too was a trap—

I think of our lives—Walt—and they work something like this—
After the aquarium moved from the Battery
to Coney Island—where you raced up and down
on the sand—and declaimed Homer to the surf
and the seagulls—my kids and I looked at the brown
sheen on the seals—and the suckers on the tentacles
of the octopus—A few blocks away my mother-in-law
was dying—depressed angry her life a waste—she said—
Refusing all help at the end—sliding back—
mumbling names no one—not even her husband—recognized—
she—and her world—went under—never to surface again—
Yet decades later my daughter named her daughter after
that old woman—and at the naming ceremony I read my poem
for my granddaughter—wondering what it's like to breast-feed
a child—even as I hit seventy and brood and nurse my back—

I think of our lives—Walt—and they work something like this

Your Grass
   —*B. Alkvit-Blum*

I think of your grass, Whitman,
and hear the stir of the great
stone forest Manhattan.

(translated from the Yiddish)

If only my mother had eaten Leaves of Grass...

If only my mother had eaten *Leaves of Grass* when I was hunched in
 her womb
I'd have come out of her a poet crying "I Sing the Body Electric"
and "Out of the Cradle Endlessly Rocking"—I'd have arrived into life
 chanting antiphonies of my selves—
with all those parallelisms and participles propelling Whitman's
 lines—tooling
them forward—linking their varied integers and leaping beyond—
 merging detritus
with vision—bearing I's and voices to the remotest craters—having
 seeped into me from inception—
his poems laving me in my amniotic sac and nourishing me while I
 was drawing on the placenta and her blood—
and on entering life I would have been an entirely different person
 from the one I became—
for if only my mother had eaten *Leaves of Grass* and it had entered me
 through the yolk sac
I would have been bold enough to approach the girl who walked the
 halls of P.S. 244
with a little red mark on each calf brought about by the chafe of the
 black galoshes
she wore to school on rainy days—and years later I would have been
 able to show a woman I loved and doubted
the quandaries of my heart—unafraid to admit all the contradictions
 jostling there—
and I would have won her—early on conceiving poems and
 warranting ideas in the tenor of my own life—
my ideas no longer the carapace protecting me from the touch of
 others
but extensions and openings and bonds—the stirrings and makings
 of camaraderie—
if only my mother had eaten *Leaves of Grass* when I was hunched in
 her womb—
but she didn't swallow any book as far as I know—not even sheet
 music or pulp fiction—
just the life she lived as the daughter of an immigrant who fled Kovno

          to escape the Czar's army
and became a drunk and shiftless carpenter in the slums of
          Elizabeth—
just the life she lived as the daughter of a mother who spoke only
          Yiddish and had to raise
five daughters on the money a bartender's kind wife wheedled from
          my grandfather
and secretly passed on to my grandmother to keep the house going
          and the girls dressed—
just the life she lived within her mother's fears—into her old age
resenting her sisters who dumped their aging mother in our small
          apartment—
and this is how I came upon the mystery of Europe through
          Grandma's jargon and her glass of tea and her stray tales and
          sullenness—
and this is how we came to deal the cards and match our hands on
          the kitchen table—
and this is how we sat in the rooms where I learned to stutter—aching
          for the fullness of words—
and this is how I became ashamed when buying bread—employing
          the tricks of pauses and elisions and elongations
and additions and rhythms and substitutions and omissions yet
          always stuckstuckstuckstuck

O Mother—I'm not glad you inherited your mother's fears—your
          intake of her
long before you knew it had happened—long before you knew she
          was inside of you—
but I am glad now—at long last—that you didn't eat *Leaves of Grass* or
          any other book
when I was inside of you and that I came out of you without a book in
          me
except the one I had to write over and over and found I could and I
          couldn't—
exactly what Whitman had to find out for himself—and so you see
          without your eating *Leaves of Grass*

you carried me home through the streets of Brooklyn—over
........cobblestone and macadam—over curb and flagstone—up
........stoop and stairway—over mat and sill—
where I would eventually sit at the kitchen table just a few feet away
........from the pilot light on the stove
and play with Grandma her special brand of casino—"steal the old
........man's bundle"—
and there we invented our own language—neither English
........nor Yiddish—yoked to each other's world—
................finding a speech for ourselves

Visiting My Father's Grave

I dig,
set down my spade
and cradle-in the juniper bush.

The worms crawl in,
the worms crawl out,
through the kishkes
and out the mouth.

But how could they come out of you?
You, tight in the coffin,
snug in the wood.
You, sealed from the dirt,
boxed from the grass.

I never threw myself upon your breast.
I never clung to you so you couldn't unloose me.
I never held you firm till you answered me something.
I never touched your lips as I touch those I love.
You never breathed to me the secret of your murmurings.

If you came back
and I were child
we'd still be apart.

What we lacked we lacked together.

Streets

Walt, I think of you on the open roads of Brooklyn, moving
from one house to another, toward *Leaves of Grass,*
writing on Myrtle Ave., then on Cumberland St.,
then on another lot on Cumberland,
and then onto Skillman St., and onto Ryerson,
and then Classon—even further out along Myrtle.
And there on Classon, in the attic bedroom
you shared with your feeble-minded brother, Eddie,
the unmade bed retaining the impressions
of your bodies, the chamber pot peering out
from under the bed, you wrote still more,
adding, re-arranging, omitting, concealing.
Walt, your faces make an album of beards.

Perhaps you became most yourself
while nursing soldiers in Washington,
your tender one-man hospice
eventually draining you as poet and man,
undercutting your health even as you realized
how touching and soothing camaraderie could be.
You learned you could flesh-out your words at the price
of your skill at making them; finally at Camden
your face more and more hidden under all that hair,
you turned into some Moses Marx Castro—
a placard of opinions, your own Whitman sampler.

But there was a time in Brooklyn when change was for you "the
    raw material of inwardness,"
and language was the laboratory in which you changed, that
    siphoned chemistry where personhood finds its word.
But, Walt, if the language of the poem is the instrument of the
    self,
how does that language re-enter and re-make the maker,
who then makes even more language out of himself?

Why, it's like moving from Myrtle to Cumberland and
then onto another place on Cumberland, then to Ryerson and
 Classon
(even further out on Myrtle), finally seeping into the central
 densities
of the borough, where we first met in a storefront library and I
 took you home with me on Utica Avenue,
on Utica Avenue, where the trolley ran all the way to the
 Williamsburg Bridge,
curving onto Broadway, under the el, and even crossing Myrtle.
And riding from the center of Brooklyn to the East River
I read you while sitting on those dark brown shellacked seats,
at the end of the line their backs pulled across the seats
so the riders could face the other way—when the trolley went
 from the bridge
toward our apartment above my father's shoe store.

With no idea of all you hid behind and hazarded out from,
I still must have had inklings, like the Morse code light on the
 cobblestones under the el.
You roamed out from those streets where you lived,
out from the houses, the rooms, the beds, the stoops,
you and your poems finally making their way to me.
And so, Walt, this sixty year birthing between us is almost over—
I arriving out of you, you arriving out of me—our mating over
 the years—
Walt, what I longed for, lacked, feared I could touch, and then
 did—you.

To America
    —H. Leivick

It's been forty-one years now that I've lived between your borders,
    America,
and have carried within me the fruits of your freedom
consecrated and blessed by the sacrificial blood of Lincoln
and the hymns of Walt Whitman. Yet see—how strange, that I'm still
    looking
for an answer to my contradictions, to the unrest of my life,
and I ask myself: why is it that up to now I haven't sung to you
in joy, in praise, in pure admiration,
in accord with your spaciousness, your states, your byways,
your prairies and your mountains and valleys, and, even more,
my four small walls—when I lived in Brownsville, or on Clinton St.,
or in Boro Park, or in the Bronx, or in the Heights;
and most of all: the many times I strolled along East Broadway—
that East Broadway that even now excites me
with tribal intimations the minute I step on its streets.

It's been forty-one years now that I've lived under your skies,
and for more than thirty of them I've been a citizen,
yet, until today I couldn't find in myself either the words
or the means to describe my arrival, my taking root in your land,
to describe the expanding revelation that you are, America.
As soon as I was about to speak to you, I hemmed in my words,
made them rigid, kept them in check,
bound them in tight-fisted knots, my whole world and my whole life
hidden under secret locks, far from your wide latitudes.
Now I must confess something to you: When I disembarked
forty-one years ago and stepped on your earth, I wanted
to fall down and kiss you. Yes, yes—I wanted to, and I should have,
but I didn't do it… Later, on your blessed earth,
and in memory of my father, I wrote poems of guilt and longing,
and I said to his spirit: "Even as late as it is, accept
my kisses that ever since childhood I wanted to give you, that I should
    have given you;

but I was ashamed to kiss you"… and even in your greatness, America,
surely you won't insist that you are more to me, closer to me, than
    my own father.

And perhaps you will reply: "I am not more, but am I any less
    deserving?"
Actually, I would love to hear you say this,
because to hear it is soothing to my heart,
and I would like to be able, even in the sunset of my days,
to unlock those confessions I've kept from you, America.
I say once again, I've tried to do that through hundreds of hints
in stanza and rhyme, in the pace of tragic dialogue,
in the rising and falling of a curtain. Again and again I've tried
to tear the curtain away from my own heart,
to become open and intimate with you, America, to be even
half as intimate as I am with the little cemetery in Ihumen,
where my father and mother lie amid far-off days,
those far-off days sunk in the deluge of World War One;
to be half as intimate as I am with the glaring snows of my tiny
    village Vittim
in Irkutsk-Yakutsk in the wilds of Siberia;
half as intimate as I am with Isaac's tread to Mt. Moriah, and with
    Mother Rachel's tomb;
with David's prayers and with Isaiah's radiant prophecy,
with Hirsh Lekert's ascent to the gallows after shooting the governor
    of Vilna,
with the dancing through the night at kibbutz Ein-Harod.
I've tried—and it's clearly *my* fault and not yours
that thirty years ago, under your skies, I grieved deeply,
complained to myself that I carry my Yiddish poems steeped in sorrow
and anxieties through your streets and your squares,
clenching my poems between my teeth the way an alley cat carries
her kittens, looking for some quiet corner in a cellar.
When I think of my brothers—Yiddish poets—
their fate grips me, and I want to say a prayer for them—wishing

them some good fortune—and immediately all my words are struck
        dumb.
Clearly, it's *my* fault, and not yours, that even today,
more than thirty years later, my heart is steeped in a new elegy;
for now, even more than before, an evil fate has flung
all Yiddish poets into new Siberias,
tossed our foundering poetry-ship into a chaos of storms,
a chaos of storms even in your waters, America,
into deadly peril; and in that very peril I seek a bold poem
of a bold captain, a bold captain who even now doesn't betray
        his fateful poem.
You see—I'm too hard on myself when I say: "Clearly, it's my fault,"
when, instead of "clearly," I'd like to say "perhaps" or "probably."
I'm trying hard not to cast any blame on you, America.
And God Himself is a witness that you are still not worthy of feeling
entirely free from guilt, entirely white as snow.
You see—you should have helped me just now to find
the right words, words that can bear nearness and fusion and farewell,
fusion with all of your beauty and all of your breadth.
Farewell?—The greater the fusion, the closer we come to imagining
the moment of parting. It can happen within your borders,
or it can happen far away, beyond your borders:
It can raise me and carry me off to those wondrous landscapes
where as a child I wandered with Father Abraham
around Beersheba, and with David around the gate of Jerusalem;
even now it can lift me to New Jerusalem.

You too, America, have walked intimately with them,
for you have also taken to heart God's command and blessing
to be a land that flows with milk and honey,
to be as abundant as the sands on the shore and the stars in the sky,
to be a prophet of freedom just as your founders dreamed you could
        be.
O, let the dream of Walt Whitman and of Lincoln also be your dream.

Now in my old age, when I stand in the clear view
of one or another bright farewell—I remember once again
that moment forty-one years ago when I reached your shore,
America, and I wanted to and I should have
thrown myself down and put my lips to your earth,
but, confused, bewildered, wasn't able to do so—
let me do it now, truly, even as I stand, embraced
by the radiance of coming closer and saying farewell, America.

September 12, 1954

(translated from the Yiddish)

A Born-Again Song of Myself

All versions issued during Whitman's life and the variants huddled in
    the margins or squeezed between lines and fleshed out to
    notebooks rose from their pages,
rose and visited me last night, keeping me awake, and I conceived of
    making the best version possible,
making a grand redaction out of all the possibilities he put before me,
    and the born-again poem came out of me;
it broke its bag of water inside of me, and the water, filthy serums,
    blood, and strange matter ran out of me,
the baby's yawp the first sound I heard after I bore down and pressed
    the poem into being,
this the fruitfulness from reading *Song of Myself* in trolley cars, in
    subways, in classrooms, in parks, in the barracks, and on the
    boardwalk,
from reading it to girlfriends I could get to listen to it,
even though I admit, O Walt, of trying to use it in place of just giving
    myself to them, bare in my desires and hesitations,
yet you too knew what it meant to disguise your loves—your coded
    names—
and I went on reading the poem year after year, as I read the Hebrew
    Bible, and Yeats, going back and back to it,
and from my rummaging in your marginalia and crossouts and
    substitutions, and from my sifting your lines, and steadily
    measuring their depths,
it became the poem we gave to each other, the poem we generated, the
    poem I
returned to you out of all the parts and possibilities you put before
    me—our composite poem—
and we sat in Camden, taking turns reading stanzas, the poem shaped
    like its first version, launching down the pages without
    sections, one long poem—our compounded poem—
and as dusk crept over the Atlantic, over Montauk, over Brooklyn, and
    came to Mickle St.,
we read our work, taking turns, our voices antiphonal,
and we were blessed, dear Walt, altered by the augmentation of our

own words in the penetrating dusk... the reading, the poem, our lives catching fire and passing between us.

(December 5, 2007)

from "Sleep-Chasings"

> *"I stay awhile away O night, but I return to you again and love you;*
> *Why should I be afraid to trust myself to you?"*
> —Whitman, *"The Sleepers"*

Poet, Ancient of Days—flying through the night sky where star-clusters
    are swirling above the fields—
the tip of your beard, wind-driven, gusting back towards your cheek,
    wedge of white hair fulgent in the night, pliant cuneiform,
a notch… a letter… a word… a language…
hairy guidon flaring out from your skin…
O standard I stare at, signaling me… longing to follow,
longing to find a clue in your body…
And then another closeup, your face reverting to the bristle hairs
disguising you on the frontispiece in '55. (O late young man
with your gamy nonchalance, your hip of dalliance, your hint of
    undershirt, your first edition.)
Come back with me now through all you wrote, to stirrings, early
    drafts, lines finding themselves, rhythms rising from delvings,
    first set of proofs,
taking me with you now, flying under your powers,
taking you with me now, flying under my powers,
I returning to you, you to me,
in this night, testing this night, trying to trust this night,
no escaping this night… or escaping you…
entering and re-entering other lives,
as my old age re-renters itself out of what came before.

from "The Last Poems of Yankev Rivlin"

I

Walt, clasping my waist, me clasping yours,
we brace ourselves, windward, near the black
accordion fence of the ferry, the Battery
resolving into detail as we head into the pier.

Walt, I too bisect V-shaped Manhattan,
jaunting up Broadway, following your urge
to flood myself with the immediate age, to
plunge into the world with my "semitic muscle."

Walt, my bootsoles jut over the curb as I wait,
their tips sloping toward the bellied cobblestones.
I gaze at the gritty glow of the felloes' rims,
abrasions of dreck glittering on wagonwheels.

II

Blowzed ancient, sanctified by your white cataract beard,
    Camden Primate
endlessly rocking in your living room on Mickle Street, site of
    pilgrimages,
that day you died, that day before I was born in Kovno, you
    finding your way there,
where I knew you early on, pocketing you for steerage to New
    York...
Song of Myself, Lid fun zikh aleyn: you, my Yiddish, my Yiddish,
    you,
you who reside both inside and outside of my rendering—*Lid
    fun zikh aleyn*—
your sounds fostering the body of my own speech, your
    Mannahatta

English whetting my Litvish Yiddish as if our speech were two
 lovers,
translation a coitus maximus, your original inciting me,
 provoking me… I
the penetrant heartened by you, translating you into a new
 tongue, and
so you see how I simultaneously possess you, lose you, deviate
 from you, seek you,
all in all own only my Yiddish even as it's infiltrating, prowling
 under your hairs,
my Yiddish extending its lines as if fingering for the skin and lips
 under all those beards of your life.

III

It's not *as if* I have finally run out of breath.
The blob of ink Beardsley said he moved around until
it turned into something glistens like a black blister.
Lamplight accents the yellow void of the legal pad,
blue pinstripes aligning vacancy from edge to edge.
Yet, I still don't know how to write about nothing.

Walt, bend closer to me in your Camden rocker. Closer.
Walt, I have become what lies under the bootsoles.
The day after you died you breathed at my birth in Kovno.
We talked on trolley cars in Brooklyn. Yesterday, the farebox
devoured my coin and we rode together from Borough Park to
 Gravesend.

Walt, the dark grass will line my throat and my mouth.

Biographical Note

Yankev Rivlin (1892-1977) was born in Kovno, Lithuania (then a part of the Russian Empire) and came to America in 1909. He lived in Manhattan, attended City College, and later on lived in various parts of Brooklyn, working for the Department of Welfare. He wrote four books of poetry: *From Kovno to New York; Coming Out From Walt Whitman's Beard; Living and Dying in Brooklyn;* and *Crossing the Atlantic: New and Selected Poems,* which won the distinguished Yankev Glatshteyn Award. He also translated *Leaves of Grass* into Yiddish.

Whitman at Timber Creek

My shirt sleeves and trousers dangle
from branches like Spanish moss. I bathe,
drag my left foot to the shore and wrestle
with the hickory sapling, thick
as the wrist of a teamster. I bend
the trunk towards me, lean as it bends away.
My wet hairs brush against the wood.
Something's hidden in the barks of trees,
within the black sockets of the birches,
within the gnarls, the burls, the knots,
behind the fringed scabs of lichen,
in the wedges of the fungi—clues to what
I feel beyond my touch. In my dream-trance
my favorite trees dance around me. A young
beech comes close, leans over me, whispers,
"Walt, it's all for you." Bodies loom at me.
I see again the mound of limbs.
Among these wood odors I smell again
the soaked gauze, see the blue face, watch
drops fall into the blood bucket. The faces
of my young men glazed over, their heads
eased off the chuff of my hand. Air
gleams within the shade of itself.
The tiniest of twigs scrawls, twists
and pokes towards me. Thickets absorb
the sundered light down to the inner
patches, down to the knobs of earth.
Proof of all I have guessed.

Richard III at the Bowery Theater
(from Whitman's *November Boughs*)

"After a one-act farce over, as contrast and prelude,
the curtain rising for the tragedy, I can see again
Booth's quiet entrance from the side, as, with head-bent,
he slowly, and in silence, amid boisterous hand-clapping,
walks down the stage to the footlights with that peculiar
and abstracted gesture, musingly kicking his sword,
holding it off from him by its sash. Though fifty years have passed
I can hear the clank and feel the perfect audience-hush.
All the performers were good in their roles, some more than one.
But the great spell cast upon the mass of hearers came from Booth.
Especially was the dream scene very impressive. A shudder went
through every nervous system in the audience; it certainly did through
    mine."

A Professor Re-reading *Calamus* (1967)

How could I have taken so long to understand you, Walt?
How could I not have known what you were about?
How could I not have seen why poetry was not enough for you?
How could I have read you and read you and not have possessed you?
I failed to take you literally, failed to take you at your true word,
failed by taking you for democratic oracle, national prophet, hymnist
    of brotherhood,
I abstracting "camerado," "companion," "brother," "lover,"
abstracting "the new person drawn to me," "the one I love," "comrade
    lover,"
abstracting "Calamus taste," "tongue aromatic," "herbage of my
    breast."
Forgive my conversions of you to professings of democracy, to
    escapist-ideals,
forgive my tenured life that failed to see all you were angling towards,
    readying for, desired.
Oh, how removed I was from all that was amorous and fluid and
    pressing in your lines,
oh, how off-base my notions about you—the evasions in my teaching,
    my book, my life—
oh, Walt, I, the teacher of reading, myself never knew how to read,
only now seeing that you even turned the dead Lincoln into the
    lost camerado.
Oh, now on the edge of retirement I become free to read you truly
    and even see
how you in all your editions and shiftings of poems and re-writings
    and omissions,
how you in all your selves' effusions and obscure hintings of an
    unrevealed life,
how you in your kaballah-like code for the initials of a lover,
how you in all your mutations and entertainings of multitudes
were giving off signs you were afraid of yourself, of being exposed, of
    being spotted behind the blinds.
So, you even misled me, as I misled myself, as you misled yourself,

we two old men ready to accompany each other, to walk the
    shoreline, where the last bubbles of spume reach our insteps.

Here's Looking at You, Whitman

That portrait of you, the one in the 1855 edition, from an engraving
 after a daguerreotype—
you don't look like a teamster, or a Missourian crossing the plains,
you don't look like "one of the roughs… disorderly, fleshy and sensual,"
you don't look like someone who's had sex with the earth or the ocean or
 the wind or his own soul.
Your right arm loosely akimbo and your left doing nothing but poking
 into a pocket,
you hardly look like someone with "polish'd and perfect limbs."
That triangle of red flannel just below the neck, pointed to by the trimmed
 beard,
summons up "I lie in the night in my red shirt," you yourself one of
 "The Sleepers."
The rumply debonair air, the slight, inviting slouch—*Walt Whitman
 depicting himself in his carpenter's garb*—you,
the intrigant, the stagey loafer—a few steps down from the *flaneur* or
 up from the drugged lounger—you,
in that "impalpable certain rest," pending, tarrying, you, in your sly posture,
sexless or multi-sexual, I can't tell which, you, coming on or waiting
 for the come-on,
you not at all like, or secretly like, the one who warns, " my firelock
 leaned in the corner,"
you not at all like, or secretly like, "the comrade of raftsmen and
 coalmen" you say you are,
you are the greatest practitioner of metamorphosis since Ovid—Demos-
 Proteus.
I actually looked for you under my Brooks Addiction Walking Shoe,
scraping the sole with a paring knife, poking, angling, among the ridges
 and smutch.
Oh, you dissembler, there and not there, yet I had an inkling of your
 approval in the lavish act of scraping the sole.
Where are you, Walt, you who disappear in the body of your poem, waiting
 for me to get inside of it?
Where are you, Walt, in that portrait of you, from an engraving after
 a daguerrotype,
you who stand atilt on the frontispiece, so openly furtive and patient?

Whitman/Vitman

If you had been Velvl Vitman, I'd have
turned your Yiddish into English, I
poking around in the circuits of your beard,
my fingers finding and tracing your face,
my palms grazing your ruddy flesh,
your body and movements affecting me
and my characters, my strokes, my lines;
the tones of the syllables, and pauses,
and the corresponding flecks of our words
make a marriage between us, my English
coming off of your Yiddish, tongue to tongue,
you then closer to me than ever before.
Or if I was Ruvn-Yankev Fayn and you still
Walt Whitman, I'd have turned your English
into Yiddish, showing how the body
of a poem could turn into another body,
the two of us closer than ever,
the way V inheres in W.

Note

"Streets" ~~ This poem quotes from and owes a great deal to Paul Zweig's magnificent study, *Walt Whitman: The Making of the Poet*. I also relied on Justin Kaplan's *Walt Whitman* and Jerome Loving's *Walt Whitman*.

Richard J. Fein's book of poems, *Kafka's Ear*, won the Maurice English Award. Two of his poems have won prizes from the New England Poetry Club. He is a well-known translator of Yiddish poetry and has published ten books of his own poetry, as well as three books of prose.

For many years he taught in the English Department at SUNY, New Paltz. He also learned Yiddish at the YIVO Institute in New York and began translating Yiddish poetry. After retiring from teaching, he moved to Cambridge, MA, spending more time writing his poetry and translating.

He was born in Brooklyn, New York, and received his B.A. from Brooklyn College and his Ph.D. from New York University. He taught at Hunter College and the University of Puerto Rico before teaching at SUNY, New Paltz. He also spent a year on a Fulbright in India, teaching American literature.

Fein's reading of Whitman goes back to his days in elementary school, and in growing up in Brooklyn he always felt a special tie to Whitman. Since 2019 is the bicentennial of Whitman's birth, Fein felt compelled to gather his poems about Whitman in a chapbook. He continues to read Whitman year after year, coming closer and closer to Whitman's poetry and to understanding the life that helped shape that poetry. Fein says, "The one poet I needed most of all to write my own poetry was Whitman."

Also by Richard J. Fein

Poetry
Selected Poems of Yankev Glatshteyn (translations)
Kafka's Ear
At the Turkish Bath
To Move into the House
Ice like Morsels
I Think of Our Lives: New and Selected Poems
Mother Tongue
Reversion
With Everything We've Got (translations)
B'KLYN
My Hands Remember
Not a Separate Surge: New and Selected Poems
The Full Pomegranate: Poems of Avrom Sutzkever (translations)

Prose
Robert Lowell
The Dance of Leah
Yiddish Genesis

www.ingramcontent.com/pod-product-compliance
Lightning Source LLC
LaVergne TN
LVHW041510070426
835507LV00012B/1461